D0205862

BROKEN CAGE

poems

Joseph P Wood

Brooklyn Arts Press · New York

Broken Cage
© 2014 Joseph P Wood

ISBN-13: 978-1-936767-29-8

Design by Joe Pan. Edited by Broc Rossell & Joe Pan.

Published in The United States of America by:
Brooklyn Arts Press
154 N 9th St #1
Brooklyn, NY 11249
www.BrooklynArtsPress.com
info@brooklynartspress.com

Distributed to the trade by Small Press Distribution / SPD
www.spdbooks.org

Library of Congress Cataloging-in-Publication Data

Wood, Joseph P. (Joseph Patrick), 1975-
[Poems. Selections]
Broken cage : poems / by Joseph P. Wood. -- First Edition.
    pages cm
"Distributed to the trade by Small Press Distribution /
SPD"--T.p. verso.
ISBN 978-1-936767-29-8 (pbk. : alk. paper)
I. Title.

PS3623.O6285A6 2014
811'.6--dc23
                        2013047700

10 9 8 7 6 5 4 3 2 1
First Edition

Acknowledgements:

The writer wishes to thank the editors of the following journals
who published these poems, sometimes with a different title or in a
different version:

anti-: Sections "On I-81" and "The belt hangs" from "End Days Suite"
Barrow Street: Sections "The overpass twists" and "My hands shake
    like boats" from "Poor Ex"
Bateau: "Stained Glass"
Bayou: "Of Anxiety"
BOMB: "The Alchemist's Prima Treatise"
Catch-Up: Section II from "Vyvanse"
Cincinnati Review: Section "Every single" from "End Days Suite"
Coconut: Sections I and VII from "Vyvanse"; Sections "From the
    lookout's steel beams" and "We has failed" from "Poor Ex"
Colorado Review: Sections IV and IX from "Vyvanse"
Denver Quarterly: "A Hot Mess"
diode: "The Afterearth"
DIAGRAM: "Shitty"
Forklift, Ohio: Section "There's no denying" from "End Days Suite"
Handsome: "Wrong"
Hunger Mountain: "Westward Expansion"
Los Angeles Review: "Broken Cage"
Memorious: "I am Ghost Brain I/ Sister to All Things Cruelty"
Puerto Del Sol: "21st Century Pleasantries"
RealPoetik: "Little Schooner"
Sink Review: "Amendment" and "Nathaniel Bacon"
THERMOS: "Baby Bear,"
Transom: Section "Better?" from "Poor Ex"
TYPO: Sections V, VI, and VIII from "Vyvanse"
Washington Square: "Clothes Unmake the Master"

"Gutter Catholic Love Song" was first published as a limited-run
chapbook from Mitzvah Chaps, 2010.

Poems from which certain titles arose: © 2011 Peter Gizzi, Threshold
Songs. Wesleyan University Press. © 2001 Jon Anderson, Day Moon.
Carnegie Mellon University Press. © 1983 W. S. Merwin, Opening
the Hand. Atheneum. © 2012 Kelli Allen, Otherwise, Soft White Ash.
John Gosslee Books. © 2012 Alexis Orgera, How Like Foreign Objects.
H_NGM_N Books. © 1968 (2007) John Berryman, His Toy, His
Dream, His Rest. FSG.

The writer cannot thank enough the innumerable writers who
shaped this manuscript in its various incarnations. Special thanks
to Elizabeth Tran and Selena Heitzman who offered me wonderful
company at Artcroft, where a portion of this manuscript was written.

CONTENTS

Part I: Variations on an Innocent Axis

Of Anxiety
13
A Hot Mess
14
Amendment
17
Poor-Ex
18
I Am Ghost Brain I / Sister to All Things Cruelty
—Peter Gizzi, "Analemma"
22
Vyvanse
23
The Afterearth
28
Clothes Unmake the Master
29
Nathaniel Bacon
30

Part II: Broken Cage

Stained Glass
34
21st Century Pleasantries
35
Baby Bear,
37
Broken Cage
39
Gutter Catholic Love Song
40

Part III: Old-New World

Little Schooner
54
When One Dance Starts, One Tongue Will Freeze
55
Lost Leiden Hymn
56
When the Ordinary Ends, a Carcass Emerges
58
The Alchemist's Prima Treatise
59
The Migraine Will Haul Itself Up / From Its Drowning
    to Find You Again —Alexis Orgera, "The Other
    Fisher of Men"
60
All Day the Moon Was a Suggestion, / A Luminous Journey
    by Night —Jon Anderson, "Day Moon"
61
Wrong
62
End Days Suite
64
Though There Was Nowhere I Had to Go / And Nothing
    I Had to Do —WS Merwin, "Yesterday"
67
Hollow. *Hollow* / Becomes an Invitation —Kelli Allen's
    "Trajectory"
68
Off in Pairs, / They Flew to Lead Fresh Lives —John
    Berryman, "Dream Song 276: Henry's Farewell"
69
Shitty
70

About the Poet

For my daughter, Daisy

Part I: Variations on an Innocent Axis

"[N]othing can be more ingeniously mischievous, more playfully sly, than this tiny trill of epigrammatic melody, turning so simply on its own innocent axis."

-Edmund Gosse, "A Plea for Certain Exotic Forms of Verse" (1877)

OF ANXIETY

Joseph, why do you shake like an egg
in quiet, why do you pontificate to the pan
like a wife, why do you hold the pen

shaking, Joseph, why do you like to edge
yourself toward minus signs—which leg
will you jam in the blender, why scan

the why's of Joseph while shaking, egg
the quiet with pontification, fry and pain
and the parachutist drowns in the reeds—

why the fascination with parting clouds
that live to part, why does the sky need
the parachutist, what drowns in the reeds

when the utility wires blacken the weeds
and kill the wiffle ball field—those sounds
aren't the parachutist or drowning in reeds—

the fascination of why, the parted clouds,
the little boy's house, the shots of mead
held in laughter, the porch lit garish save

in summertime, I remember the way I read
in the little shotgun house, bottle of mead
dumped in the garden, stealing the seed

of every failing Joseph, every slow wave
a little house of boys, the shots of mead
lit on garish Joseph laughter never saved.

A HOT MESS

Even on fire I wouldn't piss—you left me
Trembling like a greyhound—a thousand volts
In a thousand dark clouds lowering—the sea's
Left on fire—couldn't give a piss—lose me
When you ligature your waterworks—may trees
Break out in hives—closing, may my throat
Piss fire on you—I couldn't even leave me
Trembling—a thousand greyhounds—volts

Even on fire I'd never twelve-gauge my brain—
A fanciful waltz—am I wrong for dreaming—
Dickinson trembling the summer air—the same
Fire gorging—even I twiddle—never her brain—
Always one foot over the mooned precipice—
The lemmings disintegrate—a young man's game,
Firing a twelve gauge—I'll never even my brain—
A fanciful wrong—I'll waltz through this dream

Even the lemmings never—Dickinson observed—
I insist—dew destroyed chrysalis—and noted
Every single runt cub, every melted larvae
The lemmings eat—Dickinson never observed
An orgy—the trash rat alley—the dark half curve
Of neighbors' whimpered no's—O to be cloistered
In never—Dickinson even—the lemmings observed
The destroyed I and dew—*insist!* Christ notes

Every single dark stab *no* makes—an ear
Plops the quick filled guillotine bucket—
The lawn strewn—cheering families near
Every dark—the blade makes—a single err
The saints can't keep—straight to their *there*
Lies a quartered lion—a carved-up host
Makes a single dark—every stab, every ear
Fills a quick plopping—guilty cum bucket

Every quick fuck—I don't—I want—knows
The dark lawn's blades—a saint's pulled straw
Halo—jism on the breast—Dickinson glows—
For every quicky I—I don't want—fuck knows—
Kiss the wrong neck—strong, thick—brow
Not *you*—Dickinson's indecisive—clitoral call
Dark, quick want—every *I don't know*—
A dark saint—a lawn pulled—straw

Everyone say*s* *it* will get better—give me a mallet—
So long, Mr. Clock—everyone & their patience—
Neat line of bowling pins—my eyes' grey balls—
Give me *better*—everyone will say it—a mallet,
A mushroom, a missile—everyone will say *it*
Won't happen again—merlot, sun, Xanax—
Say *will*—everyone's got me—give me a melee
Long, sweet—everyone is a patient

AMENDMENT

I hate these poems
which name my breaking

down before I broke,
a lying, lived-in capitol

of cumulus and anemic
sunsets. I am tired

of parsing bell from toll—
each sound cracks me.

O regal eraser!
How you still stand!

POOR EX

We has failed. Loss is no *where*. Captured,
our hands slip apart—every word is a mountain
to diminish the other's *I*—our self a fracture
of failure. *We* is *loss*. *No* has captured
each dark clad butcher inside us. The juncture
yawns out. The future unfurls—the certain
failure is *Me*. *Loss* a new *where*. Captured,
every words slips—apart come the mountains.

Fall in a fjord and die already—be mythic
in your last air—clouds like broken teeth—
nothing's wiped clean—ground a tectonic
falling—already dying—snow—our photos drift
like the fjord's mythic collapse—quit
deed hoisted—a flag in space—between
falling and dying—our fjord ready—mythic
clouds outlast the air—I break your teeth.

Better?—*Remission?*—what's a name but a crater
whose bottom bottoms out—a buzzing some days,
a buzz-saw others—a social prosthetic—my mother
is no better—never a remission—her name a crater
I barf down deep—whoops, that's my wife—a horror
showed—she shakes my shoulders—expletives fly
like a better name, a remission of *what*—a crater
bottoming out—buzzing—whose sum makes days?

Stripped of direction—the rifle skyward—
you left me behind—blizzard of feathers:
I want to _____ you—this isn't backward—
the rifle's direction—striped sky, a ward—
strapped-down souls—moving toward
the absence of clarity—a terrible weather:
direction—stripped of the rifle—skyward
you left this blizzard—behind me, feathers.

The brainpan—here lies a gray meatloaf—
resigned like rain—some days owned me—
beneath *this*—the stalk of a thought—aloof—
here a grayed brain—the pain lies—a meatloaf:
our baby—her mobile turns—little scarves
barely warm her—never worn, her shoes—
a gray lie her brain—canned meat—loath
the resigned rain—some days own—me.

The overpass twists—a thin, dark line—*where*
are you—an inquiry defibrillated: a wolverine
mauling—*eating soup, combing your kid's hair*—
the past twists—over a thin dark, the line where
her future has retreated—an ice floe, a hard tear—
do you remember—the cup you—the one scene
in the dark—over is past, a line of thine where
inquiry fibs—dilate, I—*are you a wolverine?*

My hands shake like boats—tossed on the sea
into which I'm falling—Captain, my pills!—lost
among the inlets—babble-brained—morosely
my hands shake—tossed like a bad boat, I see
the nimbus as prediction: never to *better*—we,
Love, are done for—this house—tome or tomb,
boat or handshake—tossed into this sea
of falling pills—which, where—Captain, we're lost!

From the lookout's steal beams: a drunk coldly
billows from his mouth—he carries a snow
globe—shaking—he, I—fake flakes in a row,
we steal the others look—the drunk beams cold
radio waves—charged, we merge—and are sold
short by speech—we try to budge and tow
each other from the lookout—he steels the cold
from my mouth—billows and carries the snow.

I AM GHOST BRAIN I / SISTER TO ALL THINGS CRUELTY
—PETER GIZZI, "ANALEMMA"

It wasn't the smallpox blankets, but forgetting we gave them. How snakes wrapped our arms like vines & our hands functioned as gavels. That deep sinking feeling: us running over our convictions, the brilliant pallor of lotus leaves.

I'll tell you a secret. I died in a pothole. The water filled beyond its lip; a hideous love stretched the land. It was a mistake, the way we whinnied in our sex. Worthless pioneers, dark creek of worthless pioneers...

Angels live in our nerve endings, but always, we treat them as Martians. Where is my ray gun? Where is my skull? What knowing doesn't alleviate, I kick off like seaweed. Life without a skull is a gray cloud of meat.

VYVANSE

I.

Inside this capsule must be birdseed:
arm flap hawk gaze torso a real
cloud-lightness—jaw drop, touch cheek.
Honey, inside this capsule must be birdseed:
I can eye your eye, can rip the ragweed
out from my tongue—flooring—
Inside your capsule is that really birdseed?
Flap your arm. Gaze like a hawk. Make me sore.

II.

A verb is born—and will leave—my tongue
is not the subject. I'm an idiot—I mistook
ought to as *is*—thing about the old days: one
verb tense—*will*—begets and leaves the tongue
wanting—what?—an eternal set of whale lungs
large enough to suck the night dry—by that brook
a fawn is born into a leaf bed. Its thin tongue
subject and verb—an id it's not—no mistake.

III.

Reborn self: a blathering of *how you do you do*'s—a speech
where I explain the breakdowns, even-toned, an equation
reaching its finite end—as if friends were a faculty to teach
my mind's blathering—*do this now, don't think don't*—speech
sends them scattering. One pat on my back, their ears reach
a finite end. They take their air, eat their eats. Their relation
to themselves my utter mystery. Never blather, their speech
is even: they don't break down each breath's equation?

IV.

Tics. Tourette's. Rotten arteries. Heart valve could
erode. Mostly, a five second silence, a swarm of sand
blown inside the skull. Sniper mime: senses explode:
tick of the tourists' arteries, the boardwalk wood could
not parade its whirls more. Coked or killed, one loud
boom, the sea invades. The white light above—land
or lyre, tick or tourist, a vault is exploding—and cold,
five senses silent. Mostly swimming, the eroded sand.

V.

What are joy's forces?—how do they perform?—do they choose
which meteor molts, which face is jaundiced?—a despondence
opposes the term and composes it—if every animal were loose,
what force would bring them joy?—a hunt?—a choice
of two ducks in the bush, a turkey in the road—is the taste
a factor?—where on the chain is that appetite absent?—
what's a snail's force?—where is its ornament?—can joy choose
its face—meteor, jaundiced, molted?—is its core responding?

VI.

So great my grief? O Hardy, you should've had Facebook,
a galaxy of performative acts. We choose the wished joys
we project into space, or desperation others can overlook
and comment—give you grief or share their grief. Book
a seat to the lonesome's fast-fingered pleas—worms on hooks,
we—the also lonesome—lodge into our cheeks—toys
to our despondent cores. Jaundiced meteors, molted faces,
forces greater than performance—we can't choose joy.

VII.

A mistake: the subject enabling the verb—
I, born—never to bear—each thin bed
of mispredictions, of mores—I, curbed
by my subjects—mistake: enabling the verb
I wrote severed like a child—eyes turned
to sparrows in negative space—my head
the subject, a mistake enabled—its verb
is bare—I bore *never* in my inch-thin bed.

VIII.

Forget the equation. *We* are *they*—broke down breaths—
no blather, no speech—a microbe's job is no mystery
and its work ends too—the eclipsed, bald sun explodes—
an equation *we*—and *they*—forget. The homicidal breath
might be a gallon of space dust. Our two-block towns,
their little stores—our currency, our trinkets—memory—
an *I* or *We*—consumed in fire. The equations of breath
so much blather—give me your soul—microbe, mystery.

IX.

The sand is silent. Eroded or shoveled, heated
or frosted—the tourists arrive. These pyramids
flaunt blueprint and whip, brick and brick, feats
of erosion. The shovel never stays. The sand heats
and shifts. Misperceived, the bleached dunes seat
nothing. We carry the water, lower a camel's lip.
Silence never stays. We shovel, we ride. The heat
arrives. The tourists froth. O these pyramids.

X.

Gaze—flap—hawk soars—my arm in talon—
inside its guts, to be shitted as ten stone seeds,
a dropped whisper to the land. A day I live in
soaring, flapping, gazing—my arm its talon.
I could be the mouse or the rice field swollen
with rain. I won't remember anyone—stolen
gazes; flapping, sore bodies—my arm a talon
ripping the guts of stone, shit, seeds. I'm ten.

THE AFTEREARTH

I fall like yesterday's laundry
into the perforated life raft, among

the dead starlings, starfish,
brown kelp, cirrhosis. Plato said

Odysseus, in his second life,
will mind his own business.

The ocean like so much parchment,
we're never our own right size.

We're left with the murky waves
of brains, skipping through centuries

like a thoroughbred in a glue vat.
Our bad busted pens their razing.

CLOTHES UNMAKE THE MASTER

Too many rubies in the crown & the serfs call for your head. Purple cape fraying at the ends & the army thinks you're slack. How to state you are the State or an orb, also turn your gaze toward a beggar—make him believe you'll reattach his calf? It's tough to be like a leaf, visible veins. Harder to be the horse neck still for flies. Grow wings. Zip down to the river: the queen's voluptuous chambermaid, bare as copper. Your fingers tear the valley.

NATHANIEL BACON

Little worm busting out
a bunting's eye, Virginia

falls like second-rate
laundry. Laudanum,

O laudanum, the future
still finds me a passenger.

The boats flicker the sky
receding like a pox mark.

Who wins I cannot tell
you. Conviction is a king

with no crown, a barrel-
chested standing stood.

Part II: Broken Cage

How great my grief, my joys how few,
Since first it was my fate to know thee!
—Have the slow years not brought to view
How great my grief, my joys how few,
Nor memory shaped old times anew,
    Nor loving-kindness helped to show thee
How great my grief, my joys how few,
    Since first it was my fate to know thee?

-Thomas Hardy

STAINED GLASS

One's amber medallions evoke flies crystallized in time, but another's sharp & splintered oranges conjure half-eaten carrots. We're in Italy, where less light is demanded, but if one's eyes move from pot metal pane to pot metal pane, one would think each frame (uneven diffusion, fluctuation in shading) led to a separate universe: the bottom left, mastodons heave into myth; the center right, oyster catchers descend from an archipelago of fog. We think we know the tip-top pane: a sun exceeding sunness, starlight transubstantiated into alphabet. Friends, we are citizens of a small era, humbled lilies lilting along the hillside. The sky goes gunmetal. We own scrolls in our sleeves, testaments to miracles at such long range our minds fold.

21ST CENTURY PLEASANTRIES

My friend opens his studio's door & there's zilch on the walls,
which means he's snorting crank again. I say been keeping
yourself busy all these clumps of hair by the door. He says not
busy enough for the state council but my mother died last week
perhaps you'd answer a text or comment on my dozen status
updates on the funeral arrangements. I say motherfucker the
world doesn't hinge on your grief I was neck-deep in errands.
He says I know your goddamn kid the world is your three year
old pirouetting while singing about her latest stool sample. I
say yes among other things. Other things he says. Like voting I
say I was in the booth & mentally scraping off all the W stickers
in the state. He says how noble. I say you didn't even take ten
minutes at the elementary school to pull the lever it's only the
future. My friend says elections make me think of Lincoln &
that didn't go so well & I went there once to the Memorial I
mean I was a kid & the next day the astronauts blew up & you
could tell who were the teachers cause they all were crying. I
say what's with you & calamity you half-expect the Nazis to
reemerge bareback on a two-headed Phoenix. My friend says
this my friend is what the world calls perspective. I say no my
friend you walk like an out-of-luck leper who didn't get to go
to Hawaii back in the day & instead sat at home & stared at
his set of tops without any fingers. Bullshit my friend says it
was my idea to try to drive up to the Hudson Bay in February
but went down a snowmobile trail & found heavily bundled
hippies pining for the California harvest. I say if you remember
correctly I'm terribly allergic to that shit & besides it makes
people one slow circle of narcissism. My friends says you think
everyone's dumb like you're the one who invented the arc &
I'm Noah & lost the fucking animals & now I'm stuck with all

the cutters at the State hospital but I got news for you friend that was only for three weeks I got out fine thank you. Fine I say. Fine he says. I say who was the one who screamed at the beggar for playing *Kaddish* on a Yamaha & nodding to his phantom leg. I say who was the one who bitched about that juvie hall runaway scrawling *cunt* in the public restroom & without any explanation morphed into a tirade on the Buffalo nickel your uncle lost in a drunken stupor. I say who is the one always painting abstracts of orphanages & half-starved newborns & saying to the local Arts Weekly & I quote *I am a tissue God could toss in the air.* Shit my friend says slowly like a decade passes in the second where some dude in a tie tattooed up to his neck strides past both of us still standing in an open doorway. My friend says that guy's walking one of those hypoallergenic dogs. I say when do you think he'll get far enough up the corporate ladder he'll need to laser the tats. My friend says that guy's probably more vacant than a billboard. What would that billboard say I ask. My friend says come the fuck in I'll show you.

BABY BEAR,

Red flag on pole staked into a grass

Wind, I remember, wind in that grass
Wind through the bodies of no one I could
Wind a particular sensation I can not

Red flag on pole staked into your grass

I possess no direction utterly
What is required your sensei said that
You were small with round cheeks

And I fail, Baby Bear, fail you
How can this fact deny this thing
Brain hands hurt chest hurts deeply so
In your home
City, Baby Bear, have I utterly

On a page my body quaking
Balloon string you are the hand I am possessed beyond

What I mean is

Sensei circumstance you will if permits

You not my hand of my hand through the board
The red flag wind the more words the less is
You listen, Baby Bear, crocodiles lake wind
Like that one time
That one time

And you are
Loved beyond me which is what
Is required, afraid quake body
Baby Bear, dark choosing chose

I did not respect the deed
Every single sensation I had
Taught me whole blew these leaves
Baby Bear, I bow before the people in time
Fading never so never so one shard of
I tire take short cuts now
I don't have to finish

Everything today
Last one one last broken red sun wind knot know
Better red tape sun grass last time means know anything more
Grass grew me inside you nothing got better
I chose breaking own my I running chose me wrong run
My head hung low in my palm, Baby Bear, last this
Line grass leaves red verb who knows I you I you love love o

BROKEN CAGE

The trinity as metaphor. This is a mistake. The trinity is a static state where each part *is* the other, all equal. Mental health: pharmaceutical treatment, behavioral therapy, and—name the third. It's there: the third component is elusive and shifting, as *all* components are elusive and shifting; they evolve at their own rate, sometimes at the expense of another component.

Let me tell you a story and, months later, tell it to you again. Emotions and ideas in sudden competition. Repeat the story from an extrapolated view. Synthesize. Move forward. If it moves beyond the isolated situation—this bar, this couch, this bus stop—the little blips of emotion plant themselves in your brain's rapid-fire synapses.

That's what I want. To accept my story and become my static third. And in my trinity, dear reader, you my four-leafed clover, the anomaly in a field or knoll. I am lucky. Nothing to say about your luck.

GUTTER CATHOLIC LOVE SONG

Up on the roof, you don't think St. Barbara's on the rag or Michael's taking a piss break over behind the boiling vat of tar hitched up to the contracting truck, you think *let me raise this hammer, let me peel this loose shingle*, & it is then, my friend, you discover

how the heart seizes like a dryer exploding its gas main, how five seconds in the human world is your face gone rigid—you don't think of stones being washed clean by a stream or the broken garbage bags & rats in the alley where your friend had sucked you off,

you think *bbbbblllllllluuuuuhhhhhh*, & you fall—& if lucky recall the time you joshed your daughter by turning inside-out your eyelid, the pink undercoating slick as fish gill & her screaming at you, as she was, after all, napping, & you slapped your hands on your knees & grabbed

your sides, ironically, seeing how your body's a perfect plank, roof to street, raised up to the steaming vatlike how those divers from way up downed to the glass of milk & didn't die, so they, when you were nine, morphed into holy men, their morning

showers punctuated by patting dry with the Shroud of Turin then eating toast, molesting the butter stick, rubbing it all over their faces like cunt, & still they walked out & were cheered by their neighbors & then the moon shot out, cracked in the center, a monster Eucharist, the heavenly

body & the earthly arrived as conjoined twins, received math scholarships and strode the halls of a certain British university, laser lights where eyelashes should've been, unsheathed wires jammed into their doublewide craniums, algebra made flesh, but no one said a thing, speech being the isosceles' short side, a shoreline along the ocean's onerous acreage of doubt, where macaws on laxatives, aiming coconut-sized shits, capsize any ambitious boats of yeomen—that's what you called yourself, with a certain pride, a self-selecting serfdom, but not now, you looking all suicidal

but not suicidal, the smoking hags on stoops beating their little ones into submission, then lifting up their gazes to you like The Lord, their silence hanging between your back break on the concrete & their chorus *Call the police Frannie get some woodah get Millie oh Frances!*

& ascending a phoenix splitting into two, beaks smelted shot puts, mating calls the putter's grunt—the stadium rises as one, & as the orbs fly you fly & yet keep falling slowly, on a different stretch of land & dimension,

where airplanes have zilch for seats, souls just pile in, you & the other limbo babies or purgatory rejects sans an atom, quark, ounce of cum— the plane morphs into a plane, Muzak is piped into the stratosphere, & here's a rubber-belt assembly line where you sort of wait

saying *Hey, what the fuck, there ain't even a Wal-Mart greeter*, this is pure John Cage fantasy, this "no direction" bullshit, but an epoch passes & a headless cuckoo punctures a ceiling of eggshell-colored light—beside you, one apparition after the next diving into what's moving along the belt

like newsreels hooked up to an overworked turbine, like at the mental house, pulling an industrial-sized roll of toilet paper, & you dive into one of the fat heroin-gazed babies (as you haven't a clue whose soul you're corrupting)

& congratulations, you, Frances Nunziato Straface, are now the father tossing his daughter off the Sydney Opera House roof, now the C-Span Gavel Man, now the voice as exciting as primordial ooze, the frat boy setting fire to a thong

with an umbrella in a drink & the coed wearing it, you wield the dirt-minted shovel, weigh a sixteen-month-old who can't sit upright & fly out of the room weeping—plunging into each along the belt—conjuring Jell-O shots,

you shapeshift to a wolf, dart through the forest hinterlands, away from the choppers floating like saints but ain't saints, whores of flight, wingless birds with half-exposed tracheas, the wind & their throats a cruel chime of cartilage & this

after the school yard that very morning was mowed down by the gunman, which was not you, nor the principal, nor the palm tree trunk, nor the sirens, nor the bullets, nor the back clap, nor the rubber plant burning across the street you're learning

what you ain't, Apostolic air pumping through your narrow eyes on a street you've not yet ambulated, a crapulence of disaster undiscovered: corpses of schoolgirls in blouses & saddle shoes, St. Mary of the Assumption lapels

sewed to their chests, & the little boys, not you, in their button-up white shirts, who ran circles around base paths, jump shots with no swoosh, & the nuns who cloistered on the school steps, passing crackers like joints, those women so thick with sweater,

it's July or January & the sun might be out, you're not among them, you're late, Frances a kid caught on the same stage of Donkey Kong, the policeman by the counter examining your mis-hemmed pants, underarm holes, knee patches, your breath smells like a washer full of clothes left to sit in a pit of mold ten days, stare into that electric ape's face like he was someone who'd grab your hand & yank you into the video machine, & you would take the barrel off the maiden & rimjob her right there—no, you are left

with a snack of stale Tasty Cakes & a soft pretzel found on the pavement, the El tracks rumbling above an enormous seizure of cacophony falling squarely…but aren't there buses to sneak into, commuter trains to ride to the other side of the earth, women

who'll bare their breasts to you while their husbands hurl spears through a 900-pound pig, where if they don't boil you they take you in, teach you to grind leaves with your molars, see colors unbeknownst to dolphins & every day a new tribal virgin will wait like a dog

at the door & you'll open it & back to the Donkey Kong station—let us call this what it is: a circularity of eternity, back to the rooftop that now looks down onto a community garden the community has forgotten, where reprobates cover

themselves in cedar chips, sing songs to animals, your friends of the past now men locked to their walkers, & each falls, breaks like a Tiffany lamp, which in winter is mistaken for ice & their reputations for mastodons—what about you, your children, your wife, your baseball

card collection & the letters coming one after the other from Sicily & the priesthood you forsook & broke the Old World's heart, Olympus himself poisoning the water, going boneless in sigh, his vultures bored with their neuroses, they chant

you are the percolation of wind & wing & nail guns, you are the widow's akimbo stance at the funeral, you are the bad ideas of clouds filled with coffee, the dissected legs of fire ants, Satan's right-hand man, fetching Santa at the mall you are the charities named for the dead you know the dead don't give two licks about, you are the garbling of spices that doesn't cure the sick rooster, you are the bishop weeping by the axial bay window, you are the mortuary's tailor, you are

flagellation in a silver stain, you are your own stigmata, you've grown tired of playing the lyre while gamblers deface the world's vastest temple—you stand, flip their tables, dice scattering to ground like broken teeth, halos like Tyson upper cuts this way

& that way, the security guard on the Segway wields his illegal equipment as you don't cry *Don't tase me bro!* as every cathedral on every planet catches fire, their wine left unsubstantiated & stinking of yeast infections a boy-toy believes he can't contract

but pisses streams of nails, but everyone's laughing, but not you, you never laugh, you hover above the bong & fan the smoke out from your sea-ruby face, you prefer the sounds of ping-pong balls at night, a half-eaten cannoli, its dust of confectioners' sugar semi-

circle broken on the table, the legs about to crack in on themselves like the mule your great-grandmother rode up from a Delta levee, sharecropping best left to the freed slaves, but you say to her apparition, now an ornery parrot on your shoulder, aren't we all

the mothers & the children of indignity?, & what will burning the sugar plantation get you: an island of another country's garbage, countrymen sailing out to the Atlantic on worn-out, strung-together big rig tires— give them a boat, Frances, a yacht with sailors' caps

& inappropriate flags—crisscrossing streams between the Virgin's legs, a field of tulips where Gabriel takes the warm scythe resting up against his bare leg thick as a colt's, but he leaps into a pyramid-sized Venus Flytrap while maggots fill his horse's flanks like the fortune cookies God says you will read, & you wonder where & where the might-be met the mythic—this is the after-the-after-the-accident party you really should attend, seraphim with zebra penises piercing the sides of guests like St. Theresa of Avila, if she were in the company of zebras,

but no, she's rotting in some dark corner of heaven, picking her nails, pouring milk from a cupped fist as if it were a pitcher & the Dead Sea & its salt blocks rested inside, lick up little horsy, you have a long way to heaven's inner-gates, as they're just bullshit, a lapse of Latin, Dream

Weaver, Hebrew, Yiddish, & the television screens across the universe broadcast pigeon coops & gangsters tying notes to the right claw of the Carrier & away, another little rendezvous set in a dim restaurant, the gin going down like water,

the AK discharge like rain or pus, depending on whether you own a body—Frances, you still own one, not heavenly, not 'til you square away the daughters you left watching from the windows—ambulances wander in like drunk Shetland ponies, medics scratch their heads, pop

gum, say, *Now fella how coulda thirty-five-year-old do that to his family, plunging himself from himself, I mean, the children, I mean, what about dem bucktoothed girls up there in their bathrobes, their tears that taste like burnt spaghetti*

stuck to the bottom of the pan, ain't no drill bit nowhere gonna take that from their eyes, & he was right, in their own ways, each girl would walk into life like a fancy tea cup sporting a hairline fracture, & as age bears down, as the gravity of free will

picks again the wrong horse on a rigged track, cracks become women, one my mother and she wields a belt like a grand speech given to political prisoners—not saying I'm not fed, not saying we don't cavort over to the gravy boat, but I am an earthling adult in my house dreaming of a shotgun against my temple, my brain fluttering doves or obsidian & out of the left corner of my left eye a blob of sea-hued light, the constant thrash of waves against a small junk's aft, & you,

Frances, a drunk captain lapsing into Italian, smelling like he swallowed the stockyards of panhandle plains, Captain Frances, will we all be remade into diamonds in our due penance?—Captain Frances, the waves sound like bad ideas,

the sky a splintered shuttlecock, Captain, did I ever tell you about the dead man I found smiling in a snowdrift on that one Greenland tour, anal beads lodged up inside him, the medal of St. Christopher hung from his neck, restrained in a straightjacket,

Our Father scribbled next to a diagram of Orion, Cyrus, & the ancillary orbits of planets no one knew—I lightly kissed his frozen cheek & felt the Mongols whipping their ponies into the New World, the horses' hooves were not hooves but water skis that turned to tires

on land, Captain, where are our lances, cannons, catapults stacked with servants, breasts hanging like the goiters of sickly turkeys, why can't we fly, why are our mouths vaulted like molested children when all we want is to join the others who know the bigamous

man is the second panel in the diptych entitled "The Burning," who know intoxication should never be a guidebook on love loss, who know a fused false patina is the hallmark of a happy marriage, who know the difference

between pilgrimage & punishment is how one frames the scars—we are falling into potholes, Captain, we are down in the sewer system wrestling our amputated alligators & we are winning & gaining respect from all the wrong people—Cerberus, Triton, Dante, they all run for mayor & lose to Marian Barry, we are nowhere in the voting booth but a cardboard box above a grate, the illegal vendors selling Black Power trinkets & pirated Public Enemy T-shirts at the bus stop, you say, *Um, friend-o, let's just leave these folks*

to their bidding, & every time we pass a cathedral, you light a cigar, ponder the match, douse it & someone's hammering in the distance, you wince & I know why but we are Catholic so we never say what the problem is, not even if Christ himself

came to our breakfast nook, pulled out the nails, bled into our coffee, *Fine day for a baseball game*, Yes, *Say, what was the name of that friend?*, Dale, *No the one who got arrested for armed robbery?*, That's Dale, *Really, what happened to him?*, Well, he's in jail, Captain,

he put a .45 to someone's face & they didn't much care for it, *Is that so?*, That is so, *What are we doing here again & Please pass more creamer* & the sky through the rowhome window is all crisscrossed with telephone wires & it doesn't occur to me to phone

my mother & you'll never guess but there's much light to transubstantiate, many marriage beds to trawl from the center of the sea & every cat in every house in South Dakota has a hairball & every belfry in every bankrupt American dioceses has a weeping sniper,

Captain, coldcock me before you tenderly cornhole my boat—down it goes, I blackened among star-fish & amberjack & sharks with a dozen billion teeth half of which are sore & rotting &—I look up at the light shooting through the water & thus am saved—

you might now be among Butler's saintly directory or you might be the plankton wrapping my knee & I unfold you, I don't know nothing about rising from the sea, but someone supplies the yacht that whizzes by & nearly decapitates, but a bronzed man

in a soft tongue gives me his hand, hand towel, handshake & what
have I learned about the world that makes me want to die any less, that
makes me open my chest like a treasure vault or a toilet, depending—I
don't know how

not to blubber all over the sea lions, my flesh raw & undercooked, just as
Judas ordered & I believe in the river that every day I watch, & tonight
I believe in God, Father of the Meek, & I believe in his Light, the holes
it fills & cements & I believe in the river that every day I watch

the wind past the project's old men, their fishing poles unmoving in
the winter, the carp vasectomy-ed by ice & I believe in the house my
mother—your daughter, Captain—beat me in, one inch from a ruptured
piñata across the caved-in kitchen & I believe in my father

who ran like the Napalm girl, 17 Osborn Street, village obliterated, & I
believe in the chasm leaving a child behind creates & I believe I will shoot
my own face off before I leave my little girl to my part-time apparition
& I believe in my wife in whose heart beats a sincerity

that makes sheepherders free their flocks, astronomers swallow their
telescopes, doctors undress & X-ray themselves, I am staring down a hole
& I am at the bottom of that hole & Frances is not here now & the devil
& Christ aren't & clumps of dirt are in my palms, are my palms, hair,

penis & the fire rescue people are somewhere above arguing about a
line, it is dark, dark to the point of physical labor & I crouch down,
I've lost my harpoon, I'm just waiting on the Captain or my wife or
the neighbors to drop a pail of water or dog piss, whatever—just drop

it—the moon I'm sure is full now & teen boys tag-tackle football in the
streets & cheese steaks are crackling inside the corner store & grown
men in sports jerseys, monstrous infants with beer guts, & yes, some
smack their wives & yes, my mother is among the smacked

& the streetlights shine some of it, hide others & I'm left to piece it together here in this well, I am never going to find myself on a roof, will I Captain Frances?, I will never step out of this brain into the soft hands of maidens returning me home, will I Captain?, cuz we bomb

the meek & the invalid, the tween meth heads who quake & think of thirty-nine ways to reconstruct their faces, & their mothers, their poor mothers, never sure what to do except send them to church, say a prayer, find a friend in the pontiff, JP2 was cool, he rode in his own shielded car,

but now Vatican City is thin as a shoestring, gold gild abounds & priests march orderly & lift their faces to some imaginary light the mere earthlings shall never feel, are not commissioned to feel & so here I am, in front of St. Mary of the Assumption, the gunned-down kids arise,

thread out bullets with their fingers, return as kids playing without bloodlust, I don't know what angels do but I call them friends, & even though they beat me daily into submission & even though my mother couldn't stitch worth a damn & even though I play Donkey

Kong to avoid them, they are my blood, the pines of which comprise me & even though my mother & father live, they do so on another planet, & I wish they would change into either potted plants or fatter versions of myself, they were within your benediction, Captain Frances, but the sea

is so great & lost them in itself & so I am left to turn to you in the picture in the dream where I end myself by cracking like an egg left in a car too long, even if this hole I'm in is a roof depending which side of China you're on, I don't care, I will find a pickax

& either swing it into my throat or swing it above my head, pull myself up, step on its handle, counter-balance my feet, swing the handle again—higher, toward a light, it could be a prison, it could be an iceberg opening to reveal the scripts of answers plaguing man, swing & step, the moon is here still this morning, swing & step, I have a thousand more wounds & no one cares, swing & step, Frances I have no memory of your face on this earth smiling toward me, swing & step, the mother, swing & step,

the father, The Father, I believe in Jesus, what he did, swing & step, there are the saints, I'm ten feet from the lip of something not under something else, & now the voices are full, & now I see my wife—I see you, Amy, I see you finally—above

might be a halo & behind her broad back the river Jordan or a man suffering from gigantism or syphilis or this might not be the top at all, just dissipating mist, but I am a man, Frances, a man in your city, & I am the mist fallen

Part III: Old-New World

"And by chance Odysseus' soul had drawn the last
lot of all and went to choose; from memory of its
former labors it had recovered from love of honor;
it went around for a long time looking for the life
of a private man who minds his own business; and
with effort it found one lying somewhere, neglected
by the others."

-*The Republic of Plato*, Book X; trans. Alan Bloom

LITTLE SCHOONER

Now I the rower gentle on the water. Now I the water gentle
in refraction. If this the moon, I befuddled by its light
touch on owls, on feathers, on one bare branch settling
the rower toward stasis. If I drown, it will be in my genitals,
that dreary drooping flesh I detest—it put you in hospital
and daughter arrived to this sick, sad world. I was blighted
in my skull's noxious water. I rowed in circles gently
so as not to incur reflection. The moon insisted on light.

WHEN ONE DANCE STARTS, ONE TONGUE WILL FREEZE

Herk jerk, chicken strut—marionette pulled
Madman's spastics—mic cords quarter
The leg from the spinning—butcher cleaves

Herk and strut from the chicken—jerk pull
The tongue—jaw unhinges—jackpot falling,
Snow of coin and organ—the lead singer

Marionette, chicken herk-jerked, pulled
By wired-in spastics—madman mic, quarter
Past the dance, dance, dance—snow globe

Spills out—an embryo in a jar—bowling ball
Tumor, adipose gangrene—every frontal lobe
Dances past the past—pass the snow globe

Like a bong of skulls—wintering the cove
Of a seizure—this song's darkest syllable—
Past the dance, dance, dance—snow globe

In a spilling jar—or an embryo bowling ball
Knocking the wrong pins—betrayal spectral,
An unfurling helix—everyone says their time

Is never—jaw lock, tongue freeze—ephemeral
Betrayals—the pines are wrong—a special
Grave of tepid sun—blown brown needles—

Scratched, chipped records—a fractured hive
Pining for wrong—our betrayals spectacles
Unfurling everyone—helixes know their time

LOST LEIDEN HYMN

Little Fort, you tell me
    about myself: a sad
        marble block,

a cannon scrap. The sea
    is not my leg
        but this body

of bay strips the seagull
    carcasses clean
        of oil, grime,

daily waste
    we make to prove
        we'll never die. O

the hoop skirts and gray pants
    yellowed in a trunk,
        a trove of past

affection—the heroin
    addicts now sleep
        in the elegiac antique

store. Sun: your function
    denies your stature,
        reduction by minds

reduced by the burden
    of proclivity. You hammer
        the white out of sand,

the diamonds from water,
the walk home oranged
as reeds ghost.

WHEN THE ORDINARY ENDS, A CARCASS EMERGES

So many freaking jays—fire up the weed
whacker—unintentional melody—a shoe-
lace hops up, slices—turned the wrong cheek

to the fire—jays freak out—so many weeds
down the brown golf course—scattered seeds
on the wrong side of fate—I divorce you

from the jays—so much freaked-out fireweed—
an unintentional melodrama—wake up a shoe—
the Hindus got it right—circumstance shattered

my eye—I or it was loaded—all these holes
I never knew lace ran through—mountain bowl
of ripped-apart Hindus—circumstance shattered

in the tiptop ice—eventually our summits falter—
ocean becomes land—the first sure steps of a foal—
it rights its hinds, circumvents a rip, a shattering—

I loaded it—my eye an oar over all these holes
the tundra forgot it gave—seals wait—clubs
of slick skin—feet re-form—Viking message

clear where they stepped wrong—a word is the hub
of the tundra it forgot—we seal our wailing, club
our friends—summer sun a voracious gossip—

it reveals where my mouth falters—pins a corsage
of what I can't forget—the tundra wails—seals club
the earth's flat feet—the Vikings' message:

THE ALCHEMIST'S PRIMA TREATISE

Death blackens the crow. Burn the earth
long enough, however, and gold will burst forth
& the snow, forever squalling, will no longer be
the verified edition. For now, Apollo's Bird of

Paradise shit-smears your family's coat
of arms. Your legs, hitherto intact, burst
into rivers where the stillborn drift.
It's a borderline, astrology & the dead

you watch pyramided in the town square.
The cathedral bell tolls like it has
an extra appendage. Christ is
a hieroglyph—a tomb's rejected epitaph.

THE MIGRAINE WILL HAUL ITSELF UP / FROM ITS DROWNING TO FIND YOU AGAIN
—ALEXIS ORGERA, "THE OTHER FISHER OF MEN"

Strapped to an epileptic I spin round multiplicities of ending: a baby walrus drifting on an ice floe, a dentist's chair scorched in Mecca, a bulldozer buried beneath a mountain of clams—a grenade beats light into night, a forest of black flies.

Of course the pin is stuck—I still subscribe to earth time. Behind a pastry sign in Cyrillic, streetlights fade and the sky pinkens, a deer rustles through the trash. Life was the other way: a motion muscle makes into a prayer, a tinny music reverberating over the arboretum.

My lungs suck in the falling leaf, every petal past its smell. A rusted barrel belches fire, its crackle snaps like scissors through gift-wrap. *Were* and *Was*: a state, a place, a department of bili lights. Here's an episiotomy: the blood dries in your hair.

ALL DAY THE MOON WAS A SUGGESTION, / A LUMINOUS JOURNEY BY NIGHT
—JON ANDERSON, "DAY MOON"

The Algiers Ferry parts the cold like a substance, its passengers wounded animals common sense says to leave alone. Mist & drawbridges, the graying of fish—all October accoutrements failing to constitute a single sense.

If I approach the captain and twist his nipples and his eyelids flutter and the boat capsizes in The Big Cold Muddy, I still know nothing about his lung capacity, nothing of the nerve-mapping that made his right hand shake.

A boat is as good as its motor, just as a wildlife refuge is as good as its soon-to-be-dead or soon-to-be-born, depending if you swim or float through this life. Every day, I confuse a life vest for an anchor. Every day, the ferry chops the water like a gavel.

WRONG

If I were *Faust*. If I pissed on your grave.
If I were a mouse. The life of subjunctives.

The day turns to stone. The night a glove
of frost. If I were pissed—on your grave

alms of glue traps. What's worth saving?
Why the double take, a morning illusion,

an I for an eye? If I paused over your grave.
If I were a mouse's life. If each subjunctive

were a misfiring optic nerve. I can't live
like a sheepdog, a gentle mop of hair.

Then he busted out the window, a hive
of misfiring. Never optimistic. Can't live

ruptured, whetted—circumstance gives
no blooming now—death flowers bear

the optics of *were*. A misfiring can't live
like a sheep or a dog—congenial, moping—here

I reach for the bloodbath. Amy, we listened
to the wrong music, the late autumn strums

never had a chance. Chandeliers glisten.
Cutlery waits. Our blood, Amy, listen.

The redundancy of calendars, listen, listen.
When we are gone, we are gone. We run

for the wrong bath. Reach, Amy, listen.
The wrong autumn. A late music scrum.

END DAYS SUITE

On I-81, the valley opens wide, grassland, hills,
the cows munch over the ashes some lost oak
protects the urn a rust. It must. If you call
I-81 the valley opening grief, grassland and hills
will lose you. A vulture and the deer. A spell
of snow this trip. Each trip smells different
in the grass, a few hills, I-81, 80, 76—the hills,
the cows, munch. Here the ashes. There oaks.

The belt hangs and loops the handgun.
Xanax a sandwich bag, sunflower seeds.
Open mouth. Close eyes. You've won
a gun. The muzzle loops. The hand belts
the carnie in the face. Candy and popcorn.
Ferris wheel, bulb lit, dangling feet freed.
Stop. The shooter down, recoiled gun.
Wow, a sandwich. Jam with seeds!

There's no denying a coward his chains.
Lost in a dream, the lock unloosens itself.
Tunnels lead to beach homes. Cranes
know storms are cowards. They chain
their screeches in eternal clusters, same
five notes until the clocks are shelved—
No denying a coming. A coward chains
his loss and lock. A dream loses itself.

When should blankness be ambition?
When baseball diamonds glisten in dark.
This hole in my chest? The eternal repetition
of blankness. *When should this ambition
to collapse like a card house end?* Cessation
of self an unintended irony. *Is there a spark
in blankness, a* should *and* when *to ambition?*
When is not: a diamond, a baseball, the dark.

Every single anthracitic cell, every gut of ore
lights diffusely the broken storefronts, the brick
monuments of folly—no one here stands before
their own singed guts, their arthritic calls, or
they did, and time left them behind—the poor
remain the shattered streetlight, stars sick
in every single cell, every going gut of ore
lights diffusely the broken, storefront, brick.

THOUGH THERE WAS NOWHERE I HAD TO GO / AND NOTHING I HAD TO DO
—WS MERWIN, "YESTERDAY"

Again, before an altar to malformation, your body fits like a pajama suit—we no longer peel it, no longer finger the rain for cold. We billow like a tent. I'm bleeding through my teeth, you—who the fuck knows? I spent years white-knuckling the white line just to bury myself in shale. Now the whole shore is cleaved into the sea.

In heaven the sinners are cops, thick as colonial wedding chests, Odysseus and Ahab are brothers. I mean to say we were traveling. The lamppost doubles as a pike to place your enemy's head.

You were lonely, tired of the morning where, indeed, you'd find my head slipped inside a dry-cleaning bag. Blood on the floor, always blood on the floor. Kick my knees. Palm my kidney. It's time to play *Who cares about the dead* again.

HOLLOW. *HOLLOW* / BECOMES AN INVITATION
—KELLI ALLEN'S "TRAJECTORY"

Tonight at the meeting I confuse circumspection for introspection. I'm a monstrous infant, vacillating between *home* and *crisis*. Everyone's gaze on the floor and its hideous jewels—cigarette butts, pretzel crumbs, crumpled paper. Finally, a grizzled old-timer: *Free will isn't about the choices, but knowing you have them...I once lived in the desert and watched eagles make the same sad circles....That place, I always thought something was on the verge of exploding.*

I single-finger my name in the bathroom mirror's steam, passing gestures as speech. *Nothing is a place you can only return from again so often. To be sane is to breathe an intersection of two competing winds.* Each day atrophies, and over the course of one's life, the proverbial abacus clicks away. Click. The clay-red river. Click. Some days feel carved. Click. The herons lost in unknowing grandeur.

OFF IN PAIRS, / THEY FLEW TO LEAD FRESH LIVES —JOHN BERRYMAN, "DREAM SONG 276: HENRY'S FAREWELL"

In the rice fields beside the interstate, billboards and crows, is routine. Untenable landing starts and departure ends in a maze of kudzu and swamp. Swerving against a big rig's flanks, to screaming as the horns go crazy. The patience of a human is inductively finite. Our love didn't need to be the hue of liver failure, nor did we need to fold-in our legs like diseased deer. Every road, at some point, has a rail you can put your foot on and a chasm below, twinkling. Something snaps you upright and the road behind erodes like stomach lining. You are butchering your parallel parking. You are staring at a door, all French knockers and Byzantine window rails. The stoop, swept clean, waits for your foot. Pigeons and sparrows resume.

SHITTY

1.

Pointless not fucking you—the sun asks its course
until there's no biography—your pages stop turning
when that massive star explodes—we are gone, sources
of pointless asking—not the sun—our fucking—coarse,
cruel—frightened badgers tearing the flesh, hoarse
with rage—misnamed *passion*—our bodies spurned
on by the pointless sun—fucking you ask our course—
when *we* share a page—*until I know*—*stop turning*

2.

I know rape, I know jail. Stray nails cuts the now,
when hardened teens—ten a pack—say no friend's
here to save you—*I had hit her on the head slow*
her nails cut—I know rape and jail, a straying now
to hell with her—I am nothing inside nothing, a cow
tipped into the lake—it is dark and slimy, an end
I know straying—it's jail and nail and cuts—now
the pack grows hard—I was a teen; I had friends

3.

Attending to harm—the physician asks—*did you try*
this past year—shift and slither—*not here to judge but*—
the grass conceals the dead—still green—horse flies
attend to the ham—I ask the physician—*did you try*
that shank—two icebergs break—melting fjords slide
down my throat—*me, me, me*—the problem's heart
harms the physician's asking—*did you attend my trying*
past year—*you're not my judge*—shift and slither—*but*—

4.

Years—not the *past*—shift and slither—but do not judge
asking them—as if tired physicians—*why harm me, I attend*
to your demands—as if malady resides in a clock—a sludge
of years, we name the past—our *but*'s shift, slither, judge
what we wreck—plants, rivers, marshes—we can't budge
the soul—yes, *the soul*—to take a vacation: the white sand,
traces of shift and slither—not past nor years nor judge
nor physician—there's harm in tired asking—just attend

.

5.

When I was ten—no, a teen—it's hard to say—a friend
nail-gunned a stray cat—he's in jail now—rape—(I know
the woman)—knife in my hand, the cat hissed
*hard—I knew at ten—*NO—*when I said it, my friend—*
his mouth had this upturn—took the blade and thrusted
up the ass—organs connected pulsing, red thread—pee flowed—
I was ten, a teen—when no *was hard to say—this friend—*
in jail now—raped and cut with stray nails—I know...

6.

Autobiography stops turning its pages—or the same page
until...—pointless to ask—*you're not my fucking son—*
render that tone back—and my tone—*I choose orphanage—*
can't stop the turning—autobiography—the same page
flying on me like a demon—a hollowed-out phalange—
Sister Mary Agnes—*Go home, you don't know desperation*
*until there's no turning or stopping—*autobiography pages
a pointless asking—fuck—you are the sun

ABOUT THE POET

JOSEPH P. WOOD is the author of four books and five chapbooks of poetry, which include *YOU* (Etruscan Press) and *Fold of the Map* (Salmon). His work has appeared in venues such as *Arts & Letters Daily*, *BOMB*, *Boston Review*, *Cincinnati Review*, *Colorado Review*, *Denver Quarterly*, *Gulf Coast*, *Indiana Review*, *Prairie Schooner*, and *Verse*, among others. Wood's held residencies at Djerassi and Artcroft, and is currently managing editor for Noemi Press. He lives in Birmingham, AL.

MORE LITERARY TITLES FROM THE BROOKLYN ARTS PRESS CATALOGUE

All books are available at www.BrooklynArtsPress.com

Anselm Berrigan & Jonathan Allen, *LOADING*
Alejandro Ventura, *Puerto Rico*
Bill Rasmovicz, *Idiopaths*
Broc Rossell, *Unpublished Poems*
Carol Guess, *Darling Endangered*
Chris O Cook, *To Lose & to Pretend*
Christopher Hennessy, *Love-In-Idleness*
Dominique Townsend, *The Weather & Our Tempers*
Jackie Clark, *Aphoria*
Jared Harel, *The Body Double*
Jay Besemer, *Telephone*
Joanna Penn Cooper, *The Itinerant Girl's Guide to Self-Hypnosis*
Joe Fletcher, *Already It Is Dusk*
Joe Pan, *Autobiomythography & Gallery*
John Buckley & Martin Ott, *Poets' Guide to America*
Julia Cohen, *Collateral Light*
Lauren Russell, *Dream-Clung, Gone*
Laurie Filipelli, *Elseplace*
Martin Rock, *Dear Mark*
Matt Shears, *10,000 Wallpapers*
Michelle Gil-Montero, *Attached Houses*